Life,
Italian
Style

D1468696

Avon Books are available at special quantity discounts for bulk purchases for sales promotions, premiums, fund raising or educational use. Special books, or book excerpts, can also be created to fit specific needs.

For details write or telephone the office of the Director of Special Markets, Avon Books, Inc., Dept. FP, 1350 Avenue of the Americas, New York, New York 10019, 1-800-238-0658.

Life,

QUOTES AND QUIPS FROM

Italian

NOTABLE ITALIAN AMERICANS

Style

EDITED BY ERICA MERINO

AVON BOOKS ◆ NEW YORK

AVON BOOKS, INC.
1350 Avenue of the Americas
New York, New York 10019

Copyright © 1999 by Bill Adler Books, Inc.
Cover photograph by Armen Kachaturian/International Stock
Published by arrangement with Bill Adler Books, Inc.
ISBN: 0-380-79696-1
www.avonbooks.com

All rights reserved, which includes the right to reproduce this book or
portions thereof in any form whatsoever except as provided by the U.S.
Copyright Law. For information address Avon Books, Inc.

Library of Congress Cataloging in Publication Data:

Life, Italian style : quotes and quips from notable Italian Americans
  / edited by Erica Merino.
     p.   cm.
     1. Italian Americans—Quotations.   I. Merino, Erica.
PN6084.I73L54   1999   99-33500
973'.00451—dc21   CIP

First Avon Books Trade Paperback Printing: November 1999

AVON TRADEMARK REG. U.S. PAT. OFF. AND IN OTHER COUNTRIES
MARCA REGISTRADA, HECHO EN U.S.A.

Printed in the U.S.A.

OPM   10 9 8 7 6 5 4 3 2 1

If you purchased this book without a cover, you should be aware that
this book is stolen property. It was reported as "unsold and destroyed"
to the publisher, and neither the author nor the publisher has received
any payment for this "stripped book."

To Patricia A. Ettrick,
without whom this book would not have been possible.

Life, Italian Style

The Dream

I'm going to be a vice president at Ford before I'm thirty-five.
> —**LEE IACOCCA**, president of Ford Motor Company and chairman of Chrysler Corporation, to his fellow college freshmen

I went to vault off my toes, and the ice just exploded under me. It felt like someone was lifting me up under the armpits and then they just set me down light as a feather. . . . It was exactly how I had always envisioned it, so I wasn't sure I wasn't dreaming. It wasn't until they played the national anthem—much faster than I had imagined—that I knew for sure it was all real.
> —**BRIAN BOITANO**, figure skater, recalling winning the gold at the 1988 Calgary Olympics

I spent a lot of time in movie theaters when I was a kid, and somewhere deep down I always thought I could do it, but I never admitted it.
> —**DANNY DEVITO**, actor, director, producer

Everything is happening so damn fast. It's like a beautiful dream that never seems to end.
—**DANNY AIELLO**, actor, hoping for an Academy Award nomination for *Do the Right Thing*

Since I was two and a half and would watch [soaps on] TV, I knew I didn't want to *watch* it; I wanted to do it.
—**SUSAN LUCCI**, actress

Basically, we need to create a society in which technology is purposefully directed toward socially chosen goals.
—**SALVADOR LURIA, MD**, Nobel Prize winner in medicine for his pioneering work in molecular biology

I'll never work in a shoe factory. I have to find a way out.
—The young **ROCKY MARCIANO**, who would become world heavyweight champion on September 23, 1952

Some people's goal is to be a "movie star." I'd rather be an actor. I don't want to be bored. That's my goal.
—**JOHN TURTURRO**, actor, director

No one can take away the standing I feel I have in the game or take away my place in history. But I want to be a world champion just once before I stop. I want that ring.

—**DAN MARINO**, football player (1995)

Playing in my first World Series. Pinch yourself. Just think of all the ways to describe how good you can feel, and then add inflation.

—**YOGI BERRA**, Major League baseball player, Hall of Fame catcher, manager of the New York Yankees and the New York Mets

I had the usual dreams. I wanted to be handsome. . . . I wanted to be a killer hero in a worldwide war. . . . I wanted at the very least to be a footloose adventurer. Then I branched out and thought of being a great artist and then, getting ever more sophisticated, a great criminal.

—**MARIO PUZO**, author of *The Godfather*

If I had a single wish in all this world, it would be to give you back to you. You can make that person— you—the most wondrous, the most remarkable, the most open, the most beautiful, the most creative person in the world.

—**LEO BUSCAGLIA**, educator, author

After I knocked Joe [Louis] down with a left hook, I set him up with another one. Then I let go with my right. The punch made all my dreams come true. But it was the saddest punch of my life. How else could I feel, seeing such a great ex-champion and one of the finest sportsmen that ever lived lying there on the canvas?

—**ROCKY MARCIANO**

Last night was like a dream, and yet it happened so easily and effortlessly I have to keep pinching myself to make sure that I haven't imagined it. Last night I walked out on the balcony of the Casa Rosada in front of thousands of people and sang "Don't Cry for Me Argentina."

In the exact place [Evita] had stood so many times before, I raised my arms and looked into the hungry eyes of humanity, and at that moment I felt her enter my body like a heat missile, starting with my feet, traveling up my spine, and flying out my fingertips, into the air, out to the people, and back up to heaven. Afterward I could not speak, and I was so happy. But I felt a great sadness too. Because she is haunting me. She is pushing me to feel things.

When you want something bad enough, the whole earth conspires to help you get it.

—**MADONNA**, singer, actress

Inspirations

[Bob Hope] told me, "Come out smiling. Show the people you like them." To this day, I still follow those rules.
—**TONY BENNETT**, singer

On Monday I was in the theater, and on Tuesday I wanted to be a filmmaker.
—Filmmaker, director, producer, and writer **FRANCIS FORD COP-POLA**, on being influenced by the works of Russian filmmaker Sergei Eisenstein

He was the last reformer as mayor. For his time he captured exactly what New York City needed: somebody who can challenge the assumptions and is willing to be controversial.
—New York **MAYOR RUDOLPH W. GIULIANI**, on Fiorello La Guardia

Father Birmingham was the guy who got Bill Blatty to write *The Exorcist* and me to read Virgil.
—**JOE PATERNO**, Penn State football coach

I remember the only thing I really hungered for as a kid was [to be] the size to play baseball. When the other kids would choose up sides for a game, I was always left over, and I think that's why I went for racing.
—**EDDIE ARCARO**, jockey

The biggest thing in my early development is that my dad had a job where he could be home in the afternoon, waiting for me to get out of school. Then we would throw to each other the rest of the day. My dad keeps me in perspective. Plus, he's the best coach I ever had.
—**DAN MARINO**

Olivier's acting changed me in ways I can hardly express, even to myself. After seeing him, I could never dance the *Prodigal Son* in exactly the same way.

I had never seen anyone onstage so fully participating in every way.
—**EDWARD VILLELLA**, choreographer, dancer

People look at me and get the feeling that if a guy in a wheelchair can have such a good time, they can't be too bad off after all.
—**ROY CAMPANELLA**, Major League baseball player

The things I came to believe most deeply, I learned from the sweaty example of my immigrant parents' struggle to build a life for themselves and their children, from the Sisters of Charity at Little St. Monica's Church and from an absorbing love affair with Our Lady of the Law. They were simple values: the dignity of hard work; respect for family; respect for law and order; a shameless, bold patriotism; a recognition of the overriding importance of education; a gratitude for God's nature and a feeling of responsibility for it.
—New York **GOVERNOR MARIO CUOMO**

For me the bottom line is that handshake, that hug, that "My child goes to sleep to your music." One of

the reasons I kept going [after mom Naomi retired] was the fans.
—WYNONNA JUDD, country singer

The reason I'm in the business is when I was four-teen, I saw Clayton, Jackson, and Durante [a vaude-ville trio] at the Copa [the Copacabana nightclub], and the energy that came off that stage was like a three-ring circus.
—TONY BENNETT

[Judy Garland] educated me. . . . She educated my initiative. My father [Vincente Minnelli] gave me my dreams, but my mother gave me my drive.
—LIZA MINNELLI, singer, actress

Like the don, she could be extremely warm and ex-tremely ruthless. After my mother's first husband got killed in an accident, she got a small cash award. But the rumor brewed that she was rich. She deliberately fostered the rumor so she could pick out a prospec-tive husband. That's how she married my father. Later, my father was committed to an insane asylum.

When he could have returned home, my mother made the decision not to let him out. He would have been a burden on the family. That's a Mafia decision.

—**MARIO PUZO**, on how Don Corleone was modeled on his mother

For some reason, leather-bound copies of the goings-on in Congress lined the shelves of our living room, and I pored over them when I was twelve. I had never read anything so funny. From then on, I knew I wanted to do comedy.

—**ALAN ALDA**, actor, writer, director

My father always drilled two things into me: Never get into a capital-intensive business, because the bankers will end up owning you. I should have paid more attention to this particular piece of advice. And, when times are tough, be in the food business, because no matter how bad things get, people still have to eat. He'd opened a hot dog restaurant called the Orpheum Wiener House, and it stayed afloat through the Great Depression.

—**LEE IACOCCA**

My father was a man who'd come from a foreign country and had a hard life. He'd come back from all kinds of adversity, professional and personal. He used to say that anything that won't kill you will make you strong. What I learned from that is that you can benefit from the hard things. . . . His wisdom lies in eliminating self-doubt. His tremendous confidence, in life and in me, has been a source of incredible strength throughout my life.

—**GAY TALESE**, author of *Thy Neighbor's Wife*

Balanchine didn't leave me anything in the legal sense, but as a dancer, his ballets belong to me. In my company, we treat these ballets as if they are ours, and that is how I continue to serve my artistic father.

—**EDWARD VILLELLA**

They did this for me because I loved to skate, not because they thought I could get rich from it. They made lots of sacrifices for me but always said, "You can quit anytime you want." That freedom is the greatest gift anyone could give a child.

—**BRIAN BOITANO**

Being polite, being on time, acting in a professional manner when I was working—those things were instilled by my parents when I was very young. I give my mother and father all the credit, because they always stressed that I am no better than anyone else. At work, of course, I wanted Mr. Disney to be proud of me. He was a wonderful boss, and I valued everything he ever told me.

 —**ANNETTE FUNICELLO**, Mouseketeer, singer, actress

I don't do what my father did, but hopefully I approach what I do with the same fervor.

 —**JOHN TURTURRO**

This is where I belong. I can do this too.

 —**PIETRO DI DONATO**, author of *Christ in Concrete,* on discovering French and Russian novels

I was fortunate. I have a very great relationship with my dad. . . . He instilled in me so many great traits that, I think, I've carried on now. And I don't believe I would be who I am today without any of those regimented, instilled values and attributes.

 —Writer **VICTORIA GOTTI**, daughter of reputed Mafia boss John Gotti

I think those of us who had the privilege of being there, of being the raw material for [George Balanchine's] genius, have a debt. We have to pass that on.
   —EDWARD VILLELLA

Youth

You don't have to suffer to be a poet. Adolescence is enough suffering for anyone.
—**JOHN CIARDI**, poet

None of my relatives even knew . . . except my old priest uncle, and . . . I told him in confession so he couldn't tell.
—Auto racer **MARIO ANDRETTI**, on how his father was strongly opposed to his racing

I was sick of the game. First my dad was trying to stop me from learning the game. Now he was trying to ram it down my throat.
—World pocket billiards champion **WILLIE MOSCONI**, on why he retired from exhibition billiards at age seven

I sometimes wish that I could just say, "What do adults know?" and rebel. But I'm not that arrogant. Who am I to disregard years of experience?
—**BROOKE SHIELDS**, actress

I was sickly and even had rickets. My personality was abhorrent to other children, so I enjoyed my own company and did a lot of fantasizing. . . . I didn't have a suitable artistic outlet. Everything came out in physical challenges, like leaping from roof to roof. I had all the sensibilities of a Quasimodo in those days.
—**SYLVESTER STALLONE**, actor, writer

I wasn't a student, an athlete. I didn't have a girl. I didn't even goof off. I didn't do anything. I didn't go to the prom. I just concentrated on people. That's all I've ever been interested in. They don't give grades in my subject: curiosity.
—**GAY TALESE**

It was no great tragedy, being Judy Garland's daughter. I had tremendously interesting childhood years—except that they had little to do with being a child.
—**LIZA MINNELLI**

It was fairly insulated. I don't remember much. Whatever it was made me what I am today, and that's fine.
—SUSAN SARANDON, actress

Elizabeth Street was a facsimile, a re-creation of a Sicilian village, surrounded by Manhattan. To go to Greenwich Village, all I had to do was walk ten blocks west, but I never did it. I come from mean streets, with one foot in *Ocean's 11* and the other in *The Seventh Seal* and *Jules and Jim*.
—MARTIN SCORSESE, filmmaker, director

The town [Freehold] was on the rednecky side, and they didn't like it if you were different. Meant you had to watch out for yourself. Made getting around a lot harder. But you know, hey, I got to be me.
—BRUCE SPRINGSTEEN, singer, songwriter

In my childhood it was always two worlds. I have always felt that when you have a second language, you have three things: the first language, the second language, and the difference between them.
—JOHN CIARDI

The popular kid doesn't sit around thinking about who he is or how he feels. But the kid who is ugly, sick, miserable, or schlumpy sits around, heartbroken, and thinks.

—**FRANCIS FORD COPPOLA**, attributing his temperament to a boyhood bout with polio

It did seem then that the Italian immigrants—all the fathers and mothers that I knew—were a grim lot; always shouting, always angry, quicker to quarrel than embrace. I did not understand that their lives were a long labor to earn their daily bread and that . . . fatigue does not sweeten human natures.

—**MARIO PUZO**

It's actually random, the way you start becoming unpopular. In the third grade my girlfriend and I developed an enormous crush on a boy. It was our mission to get John germs—you know, touch the chair he sat on, collect his microbes. But after a while, he kind of got wise and resented that enormously. His friends became my enemies . . . and I became Mira Queera.

—**MIRA SORVINO**, actress

It is easy enough to praise men for the courage of their convictions. I wish I could teach the sad young of this mealy generation the courage of their confusions.
—JOHN CIARDI

I was olive-skinned in a freckle-faced town.
—GAY TALESE

I got caught stealing pencils
from the Five and Ten Cent Store
the same month I made Eagle Scout.
—LAWRENCE FERLINGHETTI, poet

Parents

I think in a way it's *everybody's* lifework to understand the relationship they had with their parents when they were very young, before they could even verbalize their feelings.
—ALAN ALDA

I resented him for dying. But you go on. If my father hadn't died, I probably wouldn't be as tough.
—Queens, New York, **CONGRESSWOMAN GERALDINE FERRARO**, the first woman ever nominated by a major political party to run for the office of vice president of the United States

My father saw [the Mafia] as bullies, as people who had to band together in order to have the courage to do things.
—RUDOLPH GIULIANI

There was no question as to who was right or wrong. There were no democratic formulas. Boom, you got knocked down. It was a good system.

—Philadelphia **MAYOR FRANK RIZZO**, recalling his father as an autocratic disciplinarian

My father . . . was always the life of the party. He wanted to make people laugh. I inherited that.

—**JOE PEPITONE**, Major League baseball player

Career and Success

I rubbed elbows with scientists and educators. Dey wouldn't shake hands wid me. So I rubbed elbows wid 'em!
   —JIMMY DURANTE, comedian; stage, screen, and radio personality

I want to thank the good Lord for making me a Yankee.
   —JOE DIMAGGIO, October 1, 1949, Joe DiMaggio Day at Yankee Stadium

Citation was the most intelligent horse I ever rode. It's a crime to take the money for riding such a horse. . . . It's a privilege and honor.
   —EDDIE ARCARO

Musicians' shoulders go back when they walk on-stage there.

—TONY BENNETT, after his 1990 Carnegie Hall concert

I look at the experience as a gift—just to have performed in the Olympics at an age when skaters used to retire.

—BRIAN BOITANO

I've never been qualified for anything I've been successful in.

—SONNY BONO, singer and congressman

I turned down more pictures than you can shake a stick at, simply because I refuse to swear in motion pictures.

—ERNEST BORGNINE, actor

It is not easy being me. I have been fighting expectations all my life, and that's a game you can never win.

—FRANCIS FORD COPPOLA

There is always some kid who may be seeing me for the first time or the last time. I owe him my best.
— **JOE DIMAGGIO**, on why he always seemed to give one hundred percent, no matter what

I was having fun. And to think that I got paid for it besides, well, that was just a plus.
— **ANNETTE FUNICELLO**, on her years as a Mouseketeer

I flourish where the action is. I like hands-on responsibility. If it works, give me the credit. If it doesn't, I'll take the rap.
— **LEE IACOCCA**

Casting directors told me I should forget about television, because I was dark. They said I might have a chance if I had blue eyes.
— **SUSAN LUCCI**

Success is the result of equal parts of craftsmanship and experience. Both take time. To acquire expert craftsmanship, the necessity of good teachers and good schools is obvious.
— **HENRY MANCINI**, composer, arranger, conductor

It's hard to remember one throw, but I'll remember the pass for the completion record, the pass for the yardage record, and the pass for the touchdown record when it happens.
—DAN MARINO

Television, everybody makes it so hard. It's painless, like taking candy from a baby.
—DEAN MARTIN, actor, singer

Working on the White House staff [Johnson administration] was the ultimate seduction. Afterwards, everything else is a tasteless passion.
—JACK VALENTI, film industry executive

It's very hard to get to the top, and it's even harder to stay there once you've made it.
—ANNA MOFFO, opera singer

The discipline is good. The discipline is important. In the end you find that if you are an actor, that's really where the fun is. The Flying Wallendas said,

"Life's on the wire. The rest is just waiting." That's your purpose. That's why I'm here. In the end, it's a plank and a passion. That's the name of the game. And as long as that's there, I'll keep doing it. When that goes, I quit. I've been pretty lucky. That's all I can say. Pretty lucky.
—AL PACINO, actor

My career is a means to my life.
—SUSAN SARANDON

I don't think I'm a bad actress. I think I've been in a lot of bad movies.
—MADONNA

I had lived around the restaurant all my life, and I like it. But Mom and Pop didn't want me in this, Mother especially; she knew how tied to it you have to be. But I don't mind not being a doctor. I'm taking care of people, but in a different way.
—VINCENT SARDI, JR., restaurateur

I don't think there's any formula to success in this business. A lot of it has to do with luck.
   —**BROOKE SHIELDS**

In that town I'm the pope. Thank God I like the song ["I Left My Heart in San Francisco"], because I sing it every night, everywhere. I don't think I've ever left it out of a show.
   —**TONY BENNETT**, on how his theme song is received in San Francisco

When I paint[ed] houses, I'd paint any color you wanted. But now I'm playing music, and I do it my way.
   —**BRUCE SPRINGSTEEN**

It was time to reposition the fashion magazine from a book of endless pages of clothes to a style magazine that readers would pick up and stay with for a few hours.
   —**GRACE MIRABELLA**, magazine founder and editor

If you're thinking of running for office, follow your instincts. You have to trust in your abilities before

anyone else can trust you. It's difficult. In all genera-
tions, we [women] still lack that confidence to seize
power and have a tendency to wait to be invited.
Don't keep waiting. Get out and shake those hands.
—Staten Island, New York, **CONGRESSWOMAN SUSAN
MOLINARI**

I've always said slower is faster, whether you're trying to come back from an injury or start a ballet
company. To succeed you must take deliberate steps
with no shortcuts.
—**EDWARD VILLELLA**

Creating fantasy is a very personal thing, but you
can't take the process—an inevitable part of which is
rejection—too personally.
—**JOSEPH BARBERA**, creator of animated cartoons

A film is a dichotomy of business and art, and there's
no other way you can figure it. And you have got to
make both work. You've got to pay attention to both.
—**FRANK CAPRA**, director, producer

I'm really hoping this [*The Tony Danza Show*] works, 'cause I'm running out of networks.
　　—TONY DANZA, actor

Our commodity is not dictated by the economy. Our commodity is dictated by need.
　　—ANTHONY DELLAVENTURA, private investigator

I rake my brain to find out why people pay me all dat money.
　　—JIMMY DURANTE

We were new to the game when we started out; we did unusual things.
　　—AMADEO PETER "A. P." GIANNINI, founder of the Bank of America, on the secret of his success

The ability to concentrate and to use your time well is everything if you want to succeed in business—or almost anywhere else.
　　—LEE IACOCCA

It's been a great life to have lived so far, and to be able to do what I love has been the greatest part of it. And it just confirms that I made the right decision when everybody told me I was crazy to start doing what I was doing.
— Singer/songwriter **BILLY JOEL**, accepting *Billboard*'s Century Award

Sometimes the best road to success is to do what other people hate to do.
— **GARRY MARSHALL**, writer, director, actor

When the reviews are bad, I tell my staff that they can join me as I cry all the way to the bank.
— **LIBERACE**, pianist

Success is not to worry too much, to do the best you can, stick to your friends and pray they'll stick to you, and let God take care of the rest.
— **JIMMY DURANTE**, as quoted by Bob Hope in Durante's eulogy.

How could I have been anything else but what I am, having been named Madonna? I would either have ended up a nun or this.
— **MADONNA**

A singleness of purpose . . . once you have agreed upon the price that you must pay for success, it enables you to forget that price.

—Professional football coach **VINCE LOMBARDI**'s definition of "mental toughness"

I'm a firm believer in taking time out to bask in my success, because everybody needs a little basking time once in a while.

—**GARRY MARSHALL**

I've reached the rediscovery period. It's a matter of time. If you stick around long enough, you end up making converts out of nonbelievers. I guess I've just worn out my critics.

—**LIBERACE**

All men are created equal. I'm just one stroke better than the rest.

—Professional golfer **GENE SARAZEN**, after winning the 1922 U.S. Open

I'm pretty ambitious. I want to try everything. I want to do whatever I can that's out there; I want to try all the different forms and play all kind of roles and just have a fascinating experience as an actor. I want to keep testing myself too. I want to live through these different experiences. I want to have a very varied artistic life.

—MIRA SORVINO

I've always believed it is a lie to think it's over when you have an abundance of creative imagination and ability. That's what kept me going.

—JOHN TRAVOLTA, actor

My life has been a series of opportunities that came rushing by. I grabbed the coattails of the horseman riding them and climbed aboard.

—JACK VALENTI

There's just no reason why you should walk into a bathroom and see a toilet. It's unglamorous.

—LIBERACE, on the fact that one of his lesser-known sideline achievements was the invention and patenting of a disappearing toilet

I am a moosician—not a doctor.
　　—ARTURO TOSCANINI, conductor, declining honorary degrees
　　from leading universities in the United States and England

It's okay to fail; just don't give people time to contemplate your failures.
　　—GARRY MARSHALL

Fame

I like being a celebrity. . . . If someone tells you he doesn't like being up there on top, you'd better look at his head.
—EDDIE ARCARO

I went from being "Geraldine Who?" to a national candidate. No matter how much you think you're this sophisticated person, there is nothing that quite prepares you.
—GERALDINE FERRARO

You make your own bed: You write a book, you go on TV, you turn around a company, your privacy goes to hell.
—LEE IACOCCA

I've been in this situation—famous—more than half my life. And I find that I like to remember the stuff *before* I became famous. More so now than ever before. There's something about that, back there, that's comforting and fun for me to go back to.

—AL PACINO

Power and fame are fragile. No one is irreplaceable or indispensable. I found that out when a president was murdered in the streets of Dallas and within minutes a new president took his place.

—JACK VALENTI

The biggest gift your fans can give you is just treatin' you like a human being, because anything else dehumanizes you. If the price of fame is that you have to be isolated from the people you write for, then that's too . . . high a price to pay.

—BRUCE SPRINGSTEEN

I never wanted to be famous. What I wanted was to be very, very good at what I do, and though I real-

ized that if I was, then I'd be famous, that always seemed a little absurd.
—ALAN ALDA

I just pinch myself now and then, to be sure it's me. And when a mob of kids appears, I catch myself looking around to see who they're running to earth. It's frightening, but it's wonderful.
—PERRY COMO, singer

I love it. I can't believe I walked into a restaurant and said to former President Bush, "I'm sorry I'm late for dinner, but I had to do *Crossfire*." That's one of those moments you want to preserve on the wall.
—SUSAN MOLINARI

Ninety percent of rock-star isolation is invented. I think a lot of people choose to withdraw from the world. To me, I go to the grocery store. It's not an issue. If somebody on the way there says to me, "Hey, I like your music," well, if that bothers you, stay home.
—BRUCE SPRINGSTEEN

There's one thing I love about myself. In New York and all over the country, the truck drivers and the cab drivers always holler at me: "Hi, Schnoz!" or "Hey, Jimmy!" I don't remember anybody callin' me mister.

—**JIMMY DURANTE**

I don't think fame's something to struggle with anymore—especially since it's so fleeting these days.

—**AL PACINO**

I've won four pennants, two World Series, managed in the All-Star game. And these women see me on the street and scream, "There goes the Slim-Fast guy."

—**TOMMY LASORDA**, Major League baseball player, manager of the Los Angeles Dodgers

I blinked and missed my own coronation.

—**JOHN TRAVOLTA**, on the fleeting nature of fame

The Craft

My painting is based on the fact that only what can be seen there *is* there. . . . All I want anyone to get out of my paintings, and all I ever get out of them, is the fact that you can see the whole idea without any confusion. . . . What you see is what you see.
   —**FRANK STELLA**, abstract painter

I wish I could tell you about methodology, but I don't know anything about it. . . . I just take my personality and put it into my character.
   —**DANNY AIELLO**

The myth has always been that after thirty-five you start to go downhill. Well, I had very good teachers. They taught me well how to preserve my voice.
   —**TONY BENNETT**

The satisfaction is in knowing you've pushed this sport, this art, to the limit.
   —BRIAN BOITANO

The most important thing about my job is to entertain. If you're not having fun, even in the most strenuous scenes, the audience isn't going to have fun. The actor can be deep, he can be philosophical, he can be dramatic, but he's got no right to be boring.
   —NICOLAS CAGE, actor

I have some general rules that I abide by religiously in selecting a story. My first rule is that it must have charm. . . . If a tale leaves you with a glow of satisfaction, it has the quality I seek. Second, it must have interesting characters that do the things human beings do—or would like to do if they had the courage and opportunity. My third and last requisite is that the members of the cast must, in real life, be the nearest thing possible to the characters they are to portray so that their performance will require the least acting.
   —FRANK CAPRA

I go into the corners deeper than most guys. I hit the brakes hard but get off them fast and onto the accelerator fast. Sometimes I begin accelerating while I'm still braking. I try to make my passes on the straightaways. The big thing is to get around the corners smooth and into the straights flat out. You try to go as fast as you can, to reach your limit and the car's limit and still stay on the track in good shape.
  —MARIO ANDRETTI

You must recognize what has to be done, and then you try to do it. It's a matter of recognition, adjustment, and execution, in that order. To play with confidence, a team must feel that everything possible has been done to prepare it fully for the coming game. Nothing's more important than that.
  —VINCE LOMBARDI, on how to build a winning team

Wine making is like movies. You start with material that's not one hundred percent in your control; then you refine what you get.
  —FRANCIS FORD COPPOLA

There can be something very poetic about violence in film. I think movies are about action—you know, bodies falling, knives sweeping through the air. That has a lot to do with what one can do in cinema so effectively.

—**BRIAN DEPALMA**, motion picture director

I usually try to find the redeeming qualities in the guys I play so that I can have a good sleep at night.

—**DANNY DEVITO**

We've always had a sound of our own. It's a pure sound. No tricks. You always know the melody.

—Band leader and impresario **GUY LOMBARDO**, on his band, The Royal Canadians

I copied Bing until I had a style of my own.

—**DEAN MARTIN**

I've been unplugged for years.

—**TONY BENNETT**, on appearing on VH-1's "Unplugged"

I always wear a jacket when I play. You just can't project the image of a prestige game in your shirtsleeves.
—WILLIE MOSCONI

You've got to be awfully careful with an actor out of work. Boosting his ego with a table in a good location is simply my way of giving him a pat on the back.
—VINCENT SARDI, JR.

My reality and film reality are interchangeable. They blend.
—MARTIN SCORSESE

I figured if [Tommy Dorsey] could do that phrasing with his horn, I could do it with my voice.
—FRANK SINATRA, singer, actor

Jumping is something I could always do, but I have . . . discovered there can't be just . . . an explo-

sion. There has to be refinement. . . . With a nice landing, the audience remembers the excitement.
—EDWARD VILLELLA

Anybody who's been at the top of a profession for ten or fifteen years without losing that edge must have something. . . . Where that edge is for sure I wouldn't swear to, but I've always thought it must be in judgment rather than in riding ability.
—EDDIE ARCARO

I see how brutal I look on the screen, but I don't know how I do it.
—ERNEST BORGNINE

To make them laugh under their tears is by far the hardest thing to do.
—FRANK CAPRA, creator of the "comedy drama"

Whatever you see during a fight is me, period. I don't know what I'm going to do. I work according to what the situation calls for, spontaneous-like.
—ANGELO DUNDEE, boxing's famed "corner man"

My uncles, my father, and my grandfather used to measure everything. The sewing was very precise. So [as a writer], I have that idea of exactitude, of not showing the work. But inside there's stitching, molding, shaping.
—GAY TALESE

[The theater is] like a garden. . . . You plant the seed; it doesn't come up right away. Sometimes it takes time. . . . *Especially* interesting is when you've done a part and you've gone off and done a movie and you come back and repeat the role. Something's happened to *you*, and it will affect the way you do a play you just did a year ago.
—AL PACINO

I spatter bits of myself all over the screen.
—MARTIN SCORSESE

Having lived a life of violent emotional contradictions, I have an overacute capacity for sadness as well as elation. . . . Whatever else has been said about me is unimportant. When I sing, I believe.
—FRANK SINATRA

I can teach technique to a talented dancer, but I cannot teach talent to anyone. Talented dancers physicalize music.
  —EDWARD VILLELLA

A policy of mine was, from the day that I started shooting with any one of the women that were opposite me, it was incumbent upon me to know a little bit about them but also know enough good about them, because if you let any bad feelings against that person be in your mind, the camera is going to pick it up.
  —DON AMECHE, actor

A pitcher can tell when his catcher lacks confidence.
  —ROY CAMPANELLA

If he flicks his ears, he's admiring the scenery or thinking about something besides running. His ears should be laid back close to his head. But the best tip-off to me is a horse's breathing. It's deep and regular when he's relaxed, but he grabs for air when

he's running under tension. Breath control is the secret of handling horses.
> —**EDDIE ARCARO**, on how a jockey tells if his mount is going
> all-out

Some dancers don't like partnering, don't like performing a service to the ballerina. But I grew to like
being a cavalier. Looking after a woman onstage,
projecting the sense of caring, of giving something to
a woman, is a wonderful, masculine feeling, and it
became one of the great sensations of my life.
> —**EDWARD VILLELLA**

A writer doesn't choose what he will write about, he
writes what comes; at least that is what a poet does.
> —**JOHN CIARDI**

If you kill off an idea too early, then you never get
to places you would have gotten to. I like very much
the imagination process. As I've gotten older, I've
found I can do it much better alone.
> —**FRANCIS FORD COPPOLA**

I'm Italian. We're all singers. Just give me a microphone, a stool, a spotlight, and a song.
   —TONY DANZA

Sometimes da difference between a good show and a bad show is jest a couple of laughs.
   —JIMMY DURANTE

Simple experiments are always best.
   —ENRICO FERMI, 1938 Nobel Prize winner in physics; considered the "father of the atomic bomb"

In its pure form, [the theater] should serve the purpose that all art serves. Art is part of mankind, an element it seems to me mankind cannot live without. It's the one element of mankind that raises it far above the beast.
   —ANTHONY FRANCIOSA, actor

The older people like the warm, personal touch, and the young audiences love the crazy clothes.
   —LIBERACE

You'll never see a crew move faster than if you say, "I've got cramps."
    —Actress and director **PENNY MARSHALL**, on her directorial method

Everything that gets into a work of art gets in by an act of choice. There may be luck, but the luck of the artist has to be earned.
    —**JOHN CIARDI**, as quoted by Donna Phipps Stout

Architects should remember they are working for beings who walk upright and resist gravity. . . . Architects should become sculptors if they want, but if they remain architects, they should embrace the wonderful limitations of their field . . . [and not seek] to surmount all of the limits all of the time.
    —Architect **ROBERT VENTURI**, recipient of the 1991 Pritzker Prize

All singers have tricks. Crosby will gargle the white of an egg. Como swallows the yolk, and I swallow the shell. Seriously, Bing just had his tonsils taken out—and I bought 'em.
    —**DEAN MARTIN**

Angling. Scheming. Creating situations. . . . That's what the kick is: stepping into the unknown and making it work for you. Believe me . . . there's nothing like it.

—ANGELO DUNDEE

If I ever tried to analyze what I do, I'd be a professional. And I'd be out of work. I'm like a fan. I get excited, I get mad, just the way a fan would.

—Major League baseball player and sportscaster **PHIL RIZZUTO**, on his trademark exclamation "Holy Cow!"

You do a lot of hard work and practice, and then all of a sudden one day the character enters you like a possession—it's as if you put on a coat and it fits perfectly. If a community-theater actor goes through the same exact steps that I do, has the same research attitude and the same interest in the subject, when we both finish, mine will be a person, and his will be something nice for community theater.

—**PAUL SORVINO**, actor

The telephone, to me, is second only to the tape recorder in undermining the art of interviewing.

—GAY TALESE

I think you're just endowed that way, born that way.
I think it's a God-given gift. That's the only excuse I
can give you.
>   —**HARRY WARREN**, "Mr. Hollywood Musical," explaining his song-
>   writing gifts

The sense of painting that we have today is formed
by the space that Caravaggio created being set in
motion by the force that Rubens supplied.
>   —**FRANK STELLA**

There's nothing more boring than being exciting, if
it's not warranted. We must remember that architec-
ture is about shelter elementally.
>   —**ROBERT VENTURI**

Don't speak to me about critics. They know noth-*ing*!
They think because the violins vibrate all the time,
they make a beautiful tone. Our NBC violins make
quick vibrato. *That* makes a beautiful tone.
>   —**ARTURO TOSCANINI**

Ballet is a human art form—it's passed on from body to body, mind to mind. . . .
    —EDWARD VILLELLA

Stagnation is death. A true art cannot live on the crumbs of the past.
    —JOSEPH STELLA

Acting

To me the whole point of acting is to experiment and learn—it's like living hundreds of lives in one lifetime.
—SUSAN SARANDON

In acting you could find some peace; you could get away from the loneliness.
—AL PACINO

It's sacred to me, acting. I know a lot of actors like to knock it because it's cool to knock it, but I don't. It's been my ticket to freedom.
—NICOLAS CAGE

One of the most difficult things about acting is synthesizing in one moment all the things that have gone on in a man's life.
—ANTHONY FRANCIOSA

[Method acting is] . . . the ability of an actor to think real thoughts on the stage. All good actors do that. . . . One advantage of the Method is that it keeps an actor from panicking. You'll never find him at a loss if he doesn't get the right cue.

—BEN GAZZARA, actor

I call it a wonderful job, working in pictures. . . . And if any actor tells you it's tough, tell 'em they're full of beans.

—DEAN MARTIN

Where I come from, you say you want to go and be an actor and they say, "What are you, crazy? You have to have a job. Make sure you have something to fall back on." I got *nothing* to fall back on.

—ROBERT PASTORELLI, actor

To wake up and know that the next thing you have to do is remember lines and say them as realistically as possible and create someone outside yourself—there's nothing better.

—DANNY AIELLO

I just found that I got paid more to say one word on *That Girl* than I did for a week of typing.
　　—PENNY MARSHALL, explaining one reason she got into acting

[Acting allows you] to totally submerge into another character . . . to do things you would never dare to do yourself.
　　—ROBERT DE NIRO, actor

You've got to mess up your body mechanics if you're going to do something different. . . . If you really want to *act*—not perform, *act*—then you have to do something different with yourself.
　　—SYLVESTER STALLONE

Work

Work is love. Work is at the heart of health.
—ALAN ALDA

I've been on sets so much that I know in the end it all
works out. People are always running around saying,
"What are we going to do? What are we going to
do?" But with effort and work, you can make it go
the way you want it. It'll happen that way.
—ROBERT DE NIRO

I thrive on work. I'm restless, worrisome, demanding,
sometimes impatient and hot-tempered. For these
characteristics, a full schedule is the best antidote.
—VINCE LOMBARDI

As I was going along, it never occurred to me that I *couldn't* do what I dreamed. I *have* had a great deal of luck in my life. But it's what I *did* with my luck that counts. It was my doing. I worked very, very hard.
—SUSAN LUCCI

I'm one of these guys—I love what I do, so I never work a day in my life.
—TONY BENNETT

We were taught that you can't wait around your whole life for people to give you things. You have to make them happen. And you make them happen through hard work.
—MARY LOU RETTON, gymnast and member of the Olympic Hall of Fame, on the work ethic instilled in her by her parents

When I enjoy what I do, I am never tired. Nothing that I like to do can be bad for me.
—ARTURO TOSCANINI

Happiness

The joy of life is made up of obscure and seemingly mundane victories that give us our own small satisfactions.
   —BILLY JOEL

All it takes is a standard song to sing and an easel on which to paint. Through song and art, I can communicate what I believe is the essence of life—truth and beauty.
   —TONY BENNETT

The *point* of all this beauty is to be happy. And I'm lucky: I am.
   —SUSAN LUCCI, at home

I'm a quarterback. I'm not a cook; I'm not a restaurant manager. Throwing is what I love to do. It brings me the most fun and the most pleasure: When someone's in tight coverage and you throw it by the guy who's covering him—like a fastball—to complete a pass. And the guy knows: He had great coverage, and he still couldn't do anything about it.
   —DAN MARINO

For a time the intoxicating joy of living as a normal man has been so great that all ambition died, too, and every hour was the exploration of a new world; . . . even death would have been a mockery for the supreme pleasure of having lived only for an hour free from the stigma of deformity. . . . This is for me truly the springtime of all life, of living.
   —HENRY VISCARDI, JR., pioneer in vocational rehabilitation for JOB (Just One Break)

Winning has a joy and discreet purity to it that cannot be replaced by anything else.
   —A. BARTLETT GIAMATTI, baseball commissioner, educator, Renaissance scholar

Marriage

All marriages are difficult—even good ones. Sharing, living together—it's difficult making room for each other. Divorce doesn't happen only in Hollywood, but the business doesn't make marriage any easier.
—DANNY DEVITO

You don't get anything for free, and the strange paradox of any long-lasting relationship is that to be fun it has to be difficult too.
—ALAN ALDA

Love

True love is wanting to give to another person without any thought about who's getting the better of the deal.
—LEO BUSCAGLIA

Love is the word used to label the sexual excitement of the young, the habituation of the middle-aged, and the mutual dependence of the old.
—JOHN CIARDI

It is when we ask for love less and begin giving it more that the basis of human love is revealed.
—LEO BUSCAGLIA

History has proven that true love is dangerous to ambitious men. . . Makes you merciful.
—MARIO PUZO

Love requires that we overcome the traditional and self-defeating fears that place distance between ourselves and others.
—LEO BUSCAGLIA

Philosophy of Life

The notion of integrity is not an academic notion. It goes to the core values of what the FBI does and what we need to do our job.
 —**LOUIS FREEH**, director of the Federal Bureau of Investigation

After being banged around so much, I'm aware that we're here by the grace of God.
 —**SONNY BONO**

Winning isn't everything, but wanting to win is.
 —**VINCE LOMBARDI**

I want to do everything, and while that may sound greedy, it really isn't. I feel that if you limit your hopes, you limit your horizons.
 —**ANNE BANCROFT**, actress

Things knock off your concentration. I have found
the simpler you get, the more complicated and rich
your thoughts can be.
    —TONY BENNETT

The only thing you can do when you're new, alone,
and afraid is to hold firm, knowing that in time you
will meet people and make friends.
    —BROOKE SHIELDS

The first time I traveled with my mother and sister
to my parents' homeland of Tonadico di Primiero, in
northern Italy, I felt as if I had been there before.
After years of looking through my mother's photo
albums, I knew the mountains, the land, the house,
the people. As soon as we entered the valley, I said,
"I know this place. I am home." Somehow I think
crossing from this life into life eternal will be similar.
I will be home.
    —JOSEPH CARDINAL BERNARDIN, archbishop of Chicago

By . . . [not hurting people], I mean not sayin' really
mean things about people and wantin' to hurt them

real bad for the sake of gettin' a laugh. An' that goes double for havin' to tell dirty jokes in your act. I've learned it ain't necessary to do that to make your audience appreciate you.
—JIMMY DURANTE

The head bone is connected to the heart bone—and don't let them come apart.
—ALAN ALDA, to a medical-school graduating class

I've always been a maverick. When I had a bobcat vest and Eskimo boots and hair down to my shoulders, my basic principles were the same—I was a maverick then.
—SONNY BONO

Managing is like holding a dove in your hand. Squeeze too hard and you kill it, not hard enough and it flies away.
—TOMMY LASORDA

Perfection is boring. I identify with people who have scars—not only on the surface—and aren't afraid to

show them. I find it uplifting that someone rises above the scars and has dignity in a bad situation.
—NICOLAS CAGE

To play this game [baseball] good, you got to be a man. But a lot of you has to be a little boy.
—ROY CAMPANELLA

If you spent your whole life doing exactly what you wanted, it would get boring. Sometimes you're going to get that call: You have to go to the dentist.
—Major League baseball player and New York Yankees manager **JOE TORRE**, during the baseball strike, as he headed for his first meeting with the 111 St. Louis Cardinals replacement players

I've got a friend who's a psychiatrist. Whenever I tell him I'm a little mixed up, he says, "Just sing." It's like the song says: "Look for the silver lining." You'll feel good every day if you look at life like that. You shouldn't regret your life. Just be happy you're alive. It goes very quick, and it's a terrific ride.
—TONY BENNETT

It's a round world, and everything comes back. So treat people the way you want to be treated. . . . Be generous and fair, not malevolent and mean-spirited.
—New York SENATOR ALFONSE D'AMATO

You want to do it right, and you don't know if you're up to it, and then what you have to do is take that first leap off the cliff into the abyss and just start flapping your wings, because otherwise you don't ever try anything.
—DANNY DEVITO

Don't confuse me with the facts!
—CONNIE FRANCIS, singer, actress

I've always been at peace with myself. If there's something that makes me unhappy, I deal with it, then I go on. I don't sit and stew.
—GERALDINE FERRARO

I have a theory that you should not get involved in politics until after you've done something else with

your life. If you get involved in politics at a young age, you lose any sense of substance and can't accomplish anything except public relations.
—RUDOLPH GIULIANI

We are vulnerable beings. We are all subject to pain and disease, and we are all ultimately going to die. The important thing is not to focus on "Why me?" but on how I can use this experience to good advantage.
—JOSEPH CARDINAL BERNARDIN

When you're in Rome, you talk Italian, when you're in Jerusalem, you talk Jewish, and when you live on the East Side, you talk tough, like everybody else talks tough, and you do the things they do.
—ROCKY GRAZIANO, world middleweight champion, TV personality

You've got to understand. I'm a Judd. My mother taught me that I'll always land on my two feet if I grit my teeth and jump.
—WYNONNA JUDD

You anticipate mistakes; get your teaching done before they happen, rather than criticizing after the fact.
　—TOMMY LASORDA

I'm not a second-place man.
　—VINCE LOMBARDI

If we play in Chicago or a little hamlet in the sticks, it makes no difference. We go all-out. No substitutes. The customers paid for Lombardo, and Lombardo they get.
　—GUY LOMBARDO

I don't care what the others think. I've always been the toughest critic of myself, and the only one I want to know me is Jesus Christ. They talk about my temper. Well, I haven't seen a good racehorse yet who wasn't high-strung. . . . Jesus Christ took a whip to the money changers, right? Well, that's a temper, and that's not a bad guy to follow. The way I see it, my temper is a great ally. It is what has pushed Billy Martin.
　—BILLY MARTIN, Major League baseball manager, former player

You have to grapple with the problems face-to-face and say, "Is it worth the trouble to make this music available?" And if you say yes, you put up with the lawsuits, the stupidity, the unkind remarks in the articles, and the rest of it. You keep on doing it, because the ultimate result is worthwhile—and it's the correct, aesthetic way to go.

   —FRANK ZAPPA, composer, rock band leader, satirist

It's important to just keep wanting whatever it is you want and fight for it, desperately.

   —SUSAN SARANDON

The secret is to hang in there. Eventually, people will respect you.

   —SONNY BONO

With this bloody life, you can't think of success, because that's not where the focus should be. There are no rewards except in what you're doing—unless you consider money a reward, and I don't.

   —AL PACINO

It is the striving to be number one that's important.
—JOE PATERNO

Looking for strange particles from here on is likely to be a kind of sport. There are other things . . . that are more important than the discovery of more particles.
—**EMILIO SEGRE**, on receiving news of having been awarded the Nobel Prize in physics

I think longevity is directly related to perseverance. I don't often get deterred.
—**BROOKE SHIELDS**

I make my living with my mind. My muscles I consider merely machinery to carry my mind around.
—**SYLVESTER STALLONE**

There's no blueprint for living. You can't say to someone, If you do this you'll be happy. Nothing like that exists. To learn things you have to experience them.
—**ALAN ALDA**

I don't have any feeling of accomplishment about something unless there's a lot of risk to it. . . . I don't want to go out there and do something three thousand other people can do.
—MARIO ANDRETTI

To a certain extent, you make your own luck. There'll be one race in which you'll get a break, and there'll be five others in which you yourself make the break. My philosophy about it is make the break come your way. It takes skill and judgment, but it's the only way to success.
—EDDIE ARCARO

So . . . who is God? He is a voice urging us to be involved in actively working to improve the world He created—every way possible, including through government. Because it is a world He loves so much that He made us so we could enjoy it.
—MARIO CUOMO

Hate makes things important, even though I think it is important not to hate.
—YOGI BERRA

A happy situation is a good situation. I don't believe in mystery.
—ANGELO DUNDEE

Dream without limit. Work hard. And know that you can turn adversity into something positive. It's like Dr. Seuss says in *Oh, the Places You'll Go!*: "You have brains in your head. You have feet in your shoes."
—SUSAN LUCCI

Compassion isn't something that you get blindly through faith. It's hard work, and it's something that you have to make a conscious decision to put into your life.
—SUSAN SARANDON

I don't set out to make a point. I set out to create understanding and compassion and present something that feels like the world. I set out to make sure something is revealed at the end of the song, some knowledge gained. That's when, I figure, I'm doing my job.
—BRUCE SPRINGSTEEN

The success in life, I think, is really—no matter where you are—a controlling of who you are so that you can actually get the best out of who you are.
—DON AMECHE

Life—regardless of who you think you are or what you believe you've achieved—touches, caresses, and smacks you around, just as it does everyone else.
—JOSEPH BARBERA

At my age if I have missed it, I probably missed it. I don't mean to sound like it is over, but let's face it, I am not about to learn how to become a shade-tree mechanic. And I am not about to see truth and beauty in the visiting team. But that does not mean that I am going to feel bad because you can tell me abut the character of wine and all I can say is it's good.
—YOGI BERRA

I don't want the job if I have to sell out. . . . It's a fun job, but if you've got to give up who and what

you are just to keep this job, then I wouldn't do that for a minute.
—SONNY BONO

It's a good thing God doesn't let you look a year or two into the future, or you might be sorely tempted to shoot yourself. But He's a charitable Lord: He only lets you see one day at a time. When times get tough, there's no choice except to take a deep breath, carry on, and do the best you can.
—LEE IACOCCA

No one gets out of this world alive, so the time to live, learn, care, share, celebrate, and love is now.
—LEO BUSCAGLIA

You may not always win, but if you know you did the best that you can do, you'll have no regrets. If you can play a sport or do something else, great, but education comes first.
—ROY CAMPANELLA

My rackets are run on strictly American lines, and they're going to stay that way.
—AL CAPONE, Chicago Mob boss

Whatever the future holds for mankind, however unpleasant it may be, we must accept it, for knowledge is always better than ignorance.
—ENRICO FERMI

You serve your country. You serve your family. You serve your God that you believe in and try to model your life after all of the principles that we learn and which we hold dear to ourselves, being someone who cares about the world around him more than in material terms or personally successful terms.
—LOUIS FREEH

Life does not have to be "perfect" to be wonderful.
—ANNETTE FUNICELLO

In everything we do, we are actuated by one motive—to build our neighborhood, our community, and our state. In that way, we are building a better America. Serving the needs of others is the only legitimate business in the world today.

—AMADEO PETER "A. P." GIANNINI

The easiest challenges are the ones you dream up for yourself—the mountains you decide to climb. The tough ones (the really lousy ones) are the ones you don't get to choose—the mountains that other people put in your way.

—LEE IACOCCA

The devil is easy to identify. He appears when you're terribly tired and makes a very reasonable request which you know you shouldn't grant.

—New York City's MAYOR FIORELLO LA GUARDIA

The quality of a man's life is in direct proportion to his commitment to excellence, regardless of his chosen field of endeavor.

—VINCE LOMBARDI

We should try to follow the advice which we often give our children. Play with your friends, be fair and honest with them, and share your toys.
—**LOUIS FREEH**, speaking against interagency turf wars

I do everything by my own volition. I'm in charge. . . . Degradation is when somebody else is making you do something against your wishes.
—**MADONNA**

What I've learned over the years is that if you start to get anxious about a situation, inevitably you'll make the wrong decision. So slow down. Investigate. And you'll feel better about the outcome.
—**JOHN TRAVOLTA**

Thank God that's over.
—**PENNY MARSHALL**'s motto

There are times in everyone's life when something constructive is born out of adversity. There are times

when things seem so bad that you've got to grab your fate by the shoulders and shake it.
—LEE IACOCCA

You just really get a strong sense of your soul. . . . I always felt pretty soulful. . . . But after that [near-death experience], it's the difference between believing you have a soul, and knowing. Because I *know.*
—ROBERT PASTORELLI

I have no regrets for what I did. I go by the saying "There's only one well on this earth, and we all drink from it." If that's crazy, then it's crazy I'm going to stay.
—FRANK SERPICO, first police officer to report and testify openly about widespread cop corruption

It's fun to disregard social dictates, but whenever you follow that behavior pattern, it creates chaos in your life and everybody else's. You can't keep a relationship and act like that wild woman.
—MIRA SORVINO

I'm not modest when it comes to my work. I have an arrogance about what is going to last. I think there are sprinters and marathon runners. I'm a marathon runner. A magazine piece is a sprint. The real test is the big book. . . . For eight or ten years you have to be willing to become unknown, not to publish, to quit, to die, and take a chance that you'll be a bust.
　—GAY TALESE

Here I am in this nice place, and I don't have to worry about where my next meal is coming from. But if I lost it all tomorrow, it would be exciting. I never like to feel too comfortable.
　—ROBERT PASTORELLI

My interest lies in my self-expression—what's inside of me, not what I'm in. And I've learned that it can't be [just about] a role. It has to be the people I'm working with and the role—maybe even more the people than the role.
　—JOHN TURTURRO

I believe that when we sleep, our soul leaves our body to be rejuvenated. Powerful and profound

things happen to us in our bed at night, and energy accumulates and hovers above it.
—**MADONNA**

I am for richness of meaning rather than clarity of meaning. I like elements which are hybrid rather than "pure," compromising rather than "clean," distorted rather than "straightforward," conventional rather than "designed."
—**ROBERT VENTURI**

I must always do only what I *feel* to do, not what I *think* to do.
—**ARTURO TOSCANINI**, recalling with regret a meeting with Mussolini

My films had to say something. . . . And regardless of the origin of a film idea, I made it mine; regardless of differences with studio heads, screenwriters, or actors, the thought, heart, and substance of a film were mine.
—**FRANK CAPRA**

When you come to a fork in the road, take it.
—YOGI BERRA

Does total creative freedom exist? . . . Yeah, you just
have to be willing to not be popular.
—MADONNA

Growth

Once, I got so mad here, I slammed this door shut hard enough that I couldn't open it again. . . . I deal with them [losses] a little better. You can't do anything about things you've got no control over.
—TOMMY LASORDA

Like many women, I've had my crises of confidence. But I have learned how to make myself heard—even in Congress.
—SUSAN MOLINARI

There is at least one must-be condition to our loving someone, and that is that he continues to grow as an individual, separately from us.
—LEO BUSCAGLIA

It was only between my senior year and the pros that I matured mentally. I came to realize that natural ability is not enough. You have to have the frame of mind that you will do your best at all times, show that you can go out there and do it. . . . It's a question of how strong your mind is, how much you want it. I've been lucky in a sense, but I found out I'm only lucky when I work hard.

—**FRANCO HARRIS**, football player

Family

My family is sacred. Nothing else matters.
   —DANNY AIELLO

Number-one records and sold-out concerts certainly thrill my soul, and I love that hour onstage. But what am I for the rest of those hours? It's pretty empty unless you have a family.
   —WYNONNA JUDD

When I was growing up in Pennsylvania, our family was so close it sometimes felt as if we were actually one person with four parts.
   —LEE IACOCCA

My first impression of family was that it was very much like a fairy tale. We were taught that Italians had a great culture. And my father was the solo flute player for Toscanini. So there was always an element of glamour and romance to my family, and to this day, if I do gravitate to them or they are the wellspring of my fondness, it's because from when I was a little kid, they were.

—FRANCIS FORD COPPOLA

Italians have more family values than anybody. The father takes care of the family; the mother takes care of the family. The children obey the parents. Nobody has family values more than the Italians, and that's why they're so good at being the Mafia. What is *The Godfather* but a heartwarming story about a family with great, solid family values? The fact that they kill people once in a while—I never show them killing good people, just bad people.

—MARIO PUZO

It could just as well be about the Kennedys, or the Rothschilds, about a dynasty which demands personal allegiance to the family.

—FRANCIS FORD COPPOLA, defending *The Godfather*

Parenthood

Raising a daughter who doesn't hate me.
—**PENNY MARSHALL**, on what she considers her greatest achievement

The night my little boy was born, it was amazing. I've played onstage for hundreds of thousands of people, and I've felt my own spirit really rise some nights. But when he came out, I had this feeling of a kind of love that I hadn't experienced before. And the minute I felt it, it was terrifying. It was like "Wow, I see, this love is here to be had and to be felt and experienced? To everybody, on a daily basis?" And I knew why you run, because it's very frightening. But it's also a window into another world. And it's the world that I want to live in right now.
—**BRUCE SPRINGSTEEN**

I often work till eleven at night and need my hug-and-kiss quotient.

—**SUSAN MOLINARI**, on how often she takes her daughter to work

No problem. I have to get up three times a night to go to the bathroom. The baby and I are on the same schedule.

—**JOE TORRE**, on having a baby at age fifty-six

Ever since my daughter was born, I feel the fleetingness of time. And I don't want to waste it on getting the perfect lip color.

—**MADONNA**

Fatherhood has added joy to my life. . . . Things seem easier to take in stride when you have a kid. The kid goes to school, and you find out what's going on, and you're involved day-to-day. It's fun. And you know, you become concerned with the future in a certain kind of way. You think about politics in a way you'd never thought about it

before. . . . *What kind of world is this? Where is it going?* And I know it's directly related to my kids.
—AL PACINO

Parenting is about feeling overwhelmed. You never *don't* feel overwhelmed. It's nonstop. *Working* is when I get my rest.
—SUSAN SARANDON

You can't let a corporation turn into a labor camp. Hard work is essential. But there's also a time for rest and relaxation, for going to see your kid in the school play or a swim meet. And if you don't do those things while the kids are young, there's no way to make it up later on.
—LEE IACOCCA

Being a mother makes you grow up and think of someone else first. In my athletic career, it was me, me, me, and achieving my goals. But when you're a mother, you can't be selfish. That's the sacrifice you make, but it's so worth it.
—MARY LOU RETTON

I just know that I will never . . . look at life the same way. And I know that I will never make another decision without thinking of her first.

—MADONNA

Children

I look at kids as little people. The little people have certain assets and liabilities. They're born with an unbounded imagination. They're born without fear and prejudice. On the other hand, they don't have the mechanical skills to do big-person stuff. But if you treat them like people, they'll learn. If you think of them as your precious little commodities and you want to mold them and shape them into something that you imagine for them, it breeds problems.
—FRANK ZAPPA

Unless there is built in a young child a sturdy moral shield, put there and fortified by parents in the home, teachers in the school, and clerics in the church, unless that child is informed by God's commandments about what is right and what is plainly wrong, unless that child absorbs and honors these teachings, then

no law, no electronic device, no so-called V-chip, no amount of speech making noisily cherished by some public officials, can salvage that child's conduct or locate a lost moral core.
—JACK VALENTI

Children reinvent your world for you.
—SUSAN SARANDON

Sometimes kids can remind you who you are.
—GARRY MARSHALL

The true function of a child's education should be the process of helping him to discover his uniqueness, aiding him towards his development, and teaching him how to share it with others.
—LEO BUSCAGLIA

Kids do look at athletes as role models. They do look up to athletes, and they follow their athletes. So, to sum it up, it's not the athlete's choice. The choice has already been made by the kids.
—FRANCO HARRIS

Of all God's creatures, a child is most vulnerable to the world. From the moment of birth and for many years after, a child is absolutely dependent upon its family—its parents and, in a large sense, the community—for the essentials of life, love and safety, shelter and nourishment. This is something that Italian-Americans have long understood: It is essential to our self-definition.

—MATILDA CUOMO, New York State first lady

Politics and Politicians

Politics is the highest vocation after the religious vocation, because the business of politics and government is to distribute the goods of the world in such a way as to improve the condition of people's lives.
—MARIO CUOMO

There can be no such thing as a right to assisted suicide, because there can be no legal and moral order which tolerates the killing of innocent human life.
—JOSEPH CARDINAL BERNARDIN

When I got elected, . . . I just adopted the rule that if it doesn't work at home, it's not going to work in

government. And it appears to me that so much of what we do would never work at home.
—SONNY BONO

Substance abuse and addiction is America's public enemy number one—not simply the nation's top health and crime problem, but like a massive oil spill off a beautiful coast, a spreading menace that fouls just about every aspect of American life.
—JOSEPH A. CALIFANO, JR., United States Secretary of Health, Education, and Welfare

I cannot think of any area where the federal government has so completely abdicated its responsibility as it has in Indian affairs. The federal agencies entrusted with administering Indian programs have clearly failed in their responsibility. Moreover, they have failed to even recognize their own inadequacies.
—Arizona SENATOR DENNIS DECONCINI (1989)

We fought hard. We gave it our best. We did what was right. And we made a difference.
—GERALDINE FERRARO

It's amazing how many comparisons there are between politics and show business, but there is an aura in politics where people feel like they have to have a certain persona and won't deviate from that or loosen up, whereas in show business they're smart enough to understand that their job is to communicate to the public, have the public communicate to them, and hopefully be liked. And I think that in that sense, we have lost touch.
—SONNY BONO

You need time to explain it to your people. If it's bad, you need time to escape it. If it's not going to be received well, you need time to cover your tracks. If it is going to be received well, you need time to go to the people and take credit for it.
—MARIO CUOMO, on the timing for passage of a bill

Disagree with us about how we distribute the pie, but agree with us that it has to be a smaller pie.
—RUDOLPH GIULIANI

Every time a school site is bought, a politician goes into the real-estate business.
—FIORELLO LA GUARDIA

The choice is not whether there will be foreign workers in this country but whether there will be legal protection or illegal exploitation of those workers.

—California **CONGRESSMAN LEON PANETTA**, during the debate over the 1986 immigration reform bill

Do you know what a conservative is? That's a liberal who got mugged the night before.

—**FRANK RIZZO**

This most liberal court . . . has embarked on a course of inscribing one after another of the current preferences of the society . . . into our basic law.

—**SUPREME COURT JUSTICE ANTONIN SCALIA**, on single-sex education

I know this society should strive for something better than what we are in our worst moments.

—**MARIO CUOMO**, on the death penalty

There isn't a Democratic or Republican way to run New York. When cities have such complex prob-

lems, they need the freedom to select the best solutions.
  —RUDOLPH GIULIANI

I don't have a political ax to grind. I'm apolitical. . . . My intention was just to have an evil opponent to play against. I don't understand why people can't take it that way—as an escape fantasy-adventure. I'm no right-winger, even if Ronald Reagan happened to fall in love with Rambo.
  —SYLVESTER STALLONE

This album contains materials which a truly just society would neither fear nor suppress.
  —FRANK ZAPPA, on censorship

Twenty years ago, someone who looked like me and had my life would not have been a legislator. I look forward to seeing how much more the world will change when we get to fifty percent.
  —SUSAN MOLINARI

I am committing political suicide. If I succeed in making this city a better place in which to live, I shall feel that the result justified the sacrifice.
—FIORELLO LA GUARDIA

As a mother trying to raise kids with some kind of a code, an honorable way to solve problems without using violence, I find it interesting to live in a country where your government is allowed to kill, whether it's war or execution. What interests me is not who deserves to die but who deserves to kill.
—SUSAN SARANDON

I never start with a political point of view. I believe that your politics are emotionally and psychologically determined by your early experiences.
—BRUCE SPRINGSTEEN

The specifications for a White House job are exacting. Anytime you play in the big leagues, they have to be. If you have a thin skin or if you balk at doing

something out of the ordinary, then the White House is not the place for you.
—**JACK VALENTI**, then Special Assistant to President Johnson

I think the one thing a politician must tie himself to is ethics. . . . You must be ethical, and you must realize that whatever you're doing, you have to do for the benefit of those ethics.
—**SONNY BONO**

Don't get the idea that I'm one of those goddam radicals. Don't get the idea that I'm knocking the American system.
—**AL CAPONE**

I wrote a song about dental floss, but did anyone's teeth get cleaner?
—**FRANK ZAPPA**, testifying before a senate subcommittee in 1985 on the influence of lyrics on behavior

Conservatives talk about volunteerism, a thousand points of light. But who provides the electricity for all those lights? The government should. The government's role should be to write the checks and stand out of the way—let private not-for-profit groups do the programs. Of course, you have to make sure the money isn't being wasted. There have to be standards.

—**ANDREW CUOMO** (1994), Assistant Secretary of the Department of Housing and Urban Development

Politics is a game of numbers. The numbers are in the votes.

—**GERALDINE FERRARO**

The issue isn't more or less government. It's dumb versus smart government.

—New Jersey **GOVERNOR JAMES FLORIO**

Pessimism and the natural instinct to raise hell are not mutually exclusive. Raising hell comes naturally to me. Still, I am not optimistic about what will happen to this country unless some radical change is made. It's going to take more than just firing a few bad guys.

—**FRANK ZAPPA**, who once considered running for the office of president of the United States

No more free lunch! (*E finita la cuccagna!*)
   —**FIORELLO LA GUARDIA**, to reporters

The Freedom of Information Act is the Taj Mahal of the Doctrine of Unanticipated Consequences, the Sistine Chapel of Cost–Benefit Analysis Ignored.
   —Supreme Court Justice **ANTONIN SCALIA**

Look at that damage and tell me that there wasn't an earthquake—a silent earthquake, perhaps, but just as insidious, just as violent, and just as harmful. And this silent earthquake has not only torn buildings from their foundations but—with a power even greater, it seems—has torn us one from another.
   —**ANDREW CUOMO**, comparing seismic earthquakes to social ones

There's a luminous quality in the movie business, but politics is mesmerizing. Both fields are unpredict-

able and full of ego-driven people whose fate ultimately depends on the public's response.
—JACK VALENTI

People are waving at me with all five fingers now.
—JAMES FLORIO, commenting on renewed voter approval while seeking reelection in 1993

The Media

Look at any country in the world, and it's easy to
see that no true democracy can exist without a free
press. But sometimes the media go too far. When that
happens, when the media place ratings, sales figures,
and their bottom line above their responsibility to
both the people they serve and the subjects of their
reporting, sinking at times into irrelevancy, they hurt
the country. How? By weakening the faith of citizens
in their government and discouraging good people
from participating. Of course, I have yet to meet anyone in the media who will admit that they ever cross
that line of responsible reporting!
—GERALDINE FERRARO

It's time for us to take responsibility for our own
insatiable need to run after gossip and scandals and
lies and rumors, to live vicariously through other

people's misery. And it's time that we realize that everything that we say and do has an effect on the world around us, that we are all connected, that we are all one, and until we change our negative behavior, tragedies like this [the death of Princess Diana] will continue to occur.
　—MADONNA

Rock journalism is people who can't write, interviewing people who can't talk, for people who can't read.
　—FRANK ZAPPA

Nosiness represents mainly the interests of the mean-spirited, the one-night-stand temperament of tabloid journalists and even mainstream writers and biographers seizing every opportunity to belittle big names, to publicize a public figure's slip of the tongue, to scandalize every sexual dalliance even when it bears no relevance to that person's political or public service.
　—GAY TALESE

Law and Order

If you can present people with the distinct possibility, even the probability, that they could be caught and that they could be held up to public shame, ridicule, and possible prison sentences, you're going to affect their behavior.
—RUDOLPH GIULIANI

I hate to say it, but crime is an overhead you have to pay if you want to live in the city.
—San Francisco **MAYOR GEORGE MOSCONE**

I don't know if it will stop violent crime by taking the life of the person who commits the vicious crime, but I am certain of one thing—that he won't be around to commit another murder.
—**FRANK RIZZO**, on capital punishment

When is it . . . that the psychotherapist came to play such an indispensable role in the maintenance of the citizenry's mental health? For most of history, men and women have worked out their difficulties by talking to . . . parents, siblings, friends, and bartenders—none of whom was awarded a privilege against testifying in court.
—ANTONIN SCALIA

These are not Holiday Inns we're running. These are the institutions where we put our most dangerous people. And a different set of rules should apply.
—Nevada ATTORNEY GENERAL FRANKIE SUE DEL PAPA

I don't think law enforcement works unless there's some basic supportive work which is not only carried on contemporaneous with the enforcement, but something which starts with three- and four-year-olds and works in a meaningful way to teach values and respect for the law and gives opportunities to people who don't have them.
—LOUIS FREEH

When I took that oath to enforce the law, it didn't say "against everybody except other cops."
—FRANK SERPICO

Religion

[Catholicism] is one spooky religion. When you reach back for mysterious or terrifying images, you're going to dredge up many more Catholic memories than Presbyterian ones.
—BRIAN DEPALMA

There's a side of me that wants to be good. But there's another side that's a little bit of a rebel. I always believed it was right to go to church, but sometimes I have this overwhelming urge to ride my Harley up and down the aisles.
—WYNONNA JUDD

To become a lapsed Catholic, first go to a Catholic university.
—SUSAN SARANDON

It was possible to do what I've done only because I escaped the bondage of being a devout believer. To be a good member of the congregation, ultimately you have to stop thinking. The essence of Christianity is told to us in the Garden of Eden story. The fruit that was forbidden was on the tree of knowledge. The subtext is, All the suffering you have is because you wanted to find out what was going on. You could still be in the Garden of Eden if you had just kept your . . . mouth shut and hadn't asked any questions.
—FRANK ZAPPA

We've tried teaching the doctrine and demanding that people follow it. It doesn't work. In the United States we have been brought up thinking that we shouldn't accept things unless they make sense to us. If we ignore that cultural dimension and just say take it or leave it on the basis of authority, some people will respond positively, but a lot will not. Jesus taught parables. But it was seldom that He said, "This is the way it's got to be." Any effort to teach solely by fear is not going to work.
—JOSEPH CARDINAL BERNARDIN

I like that ritual in my life. I appreciate that time.
—BROOKE SHIELDS, on going to church

The acceptance of this faith requires a lifelong struggle to understand it more fully and to live it more truly, to translate truth into experience, to practice as well as to believe.
—MARIO CUOMO

I don't know where the rage comes from. But it has been offset by religion a great deal. I find myself looking to keep it controlled. I'm not a practicing Catholic, but I'm constantly dealing with religion and reading about it and trying to make films about it.
—MARTIN SCORSESE

I thought confession was one of the earliest forms of invasion of privacy—earliest forms of surveillance—that I could think of.
—FRANCIS FORD COPPOLA

When Mama was alive, God rest her soul, I'd always follow her to church to find out where God is. I still follow her.
—JIMMY DURANTE

Personal religious convictions have no place in political campaigns or in dictating public policy. I have always felt that the spiritual beliefs of elected representatives are between them and their God, not their government.
—GERALDINE FERRARO

I still go to church sometimes. I say my prayers. But I feel like the kind of faith or spirituality I have is really a combination of things. Certainly there's Catholicism in there, but it's rather nondenominational.
—MADONNA

Equality

We have seen some of the fruits of Dr. [Martin Luther] King's efforts, and yet, twenty-six years later, we see perhaps even more clearly what remains to be done. But we will never again be the same as a nation because of his prophetic vision. He forced us to face squarely the moral, political, and constitutional crisis caused for us, as individuals and as a nation, by basing our political system on the principles of human dignity and equality while basing our practice on a systematic denial of those principles.
   —JOSEPH CARDINAL BERNARDIN

We've chosen the path to equality; don't let them turn us around.
   —GERALDINE FERRARO

My father came to this country when he was a teenager. Not only had he never profited from the sweat

of any black man's brow; I don't think he had ever
seen a black man.
   —**ANTONIN SCALIA**, on set-asides and preferential treatment

Quotas don't help anyone. In fact, they are one of
the worst forms of racial and gender-based discrimi-
nation. Every American citizen should be treated
equally and should have equal opportunity under
the law.
   —**ALFONSE D'AMATO**

Racism in our country and in this metropolitan area
[Chicago] is a fact. Racism is a sin.
   —**JOSEPH CARDINAL BERNARDIN**

I think my being in the room reminds them that
there's a wing of our party that's important.
   —**SUSAN MOLINARI**

In show business you learn pretty quick that people,
no matter what color or religion they are, should be
treated the exact same way.
   —**JIMMY DURANTE**

No government has the right to discriminate against any of its own citizens. That's why I support allowing gays in the military. The private behavior of individuals should not be the issue. Rather, the men and women of the armed forces should be judged by how well they perform their jobs.
—ALFONSE D'AMATO

We know now that women can run for high political office. We have proved we have the stamina to get through a campaign, to stand up for our beliefs in a national televised debate, to articulate the issues. And we have certainly proved that women are able to stand up under pressure. I don't think the press will be looking to see if the next female candidate will burst out crying every time she has a press conference. Perhaps the style of her campaign will be less important and the substance of her campaign will get the attention it deserves.
—GERALDINE FERRARO

Retirement

You start chasing a ball, and your brain immediately commands your body to "Run forward! Scoop up the ball! Peg it to the infield!" Then your body says, "Who, me?"
—JOE DIMAGGIO

I'll be the one to know when I shouldn't play anymore. People always want to retire athletes before their time, but that's not going to happen to me. Nobody's going to get me to go sooner than I want to, sooner than I believe I should.
—JOE MONTANA, football player

I'm not ending it at the top, but I'm sure as hell not ending it at the bottom, either.
—MARIO ANDRETTI

Retirement's okay if you like to chew gum. Me, I love to work, and I love to make money.
  —**JENO PAULUCCI**, builder of three major food businesses, including Chung King and Jeno's; founding chairman of RJR Nabisco

To retire is to drop. I'll never retire. I'll never lose the juice! Stick and move! . . . Each fight is new juice. Each new fighter is penicillin. I'll stay young forever because I have these challenges.
  —**ANGELO DUNDEE**

Old injuries have caught up with me, and I've had new ones. . . . I feel that I have reached the stage where I can no longer produce for my ball club, my manager, my teammates, and my fans the sort of baseball their loyalty to me deserves.
  —**JOE DIMAGGIO**, announcing his retirement as a player on December 11, 1951

It felt like a job, and that's when I told myself it would be time to leave.
  —**JOE MONTANA**

Some guys in this business slow down, retire, and take it easy. A couple of months later, they're dead.
—LEE IACOCCA

When I was managing the minor leagues for eight seasons, I used to pray to God every night. I'd say, "Dear God, if you can find it in your heart, please let me manage in the big leagues." I managed in winter ball for six more years, trying to refine my skills, and I used to pray the same way, only I had refined the prayer by then. "Dear God, I don't just want to be a manager in the big leagues; I want to manage the Dodgers." . . . You can call me corny. But those prayers were answered. That dream came true for me. It keeps coming true, because I've still got this job. And I'm not about to give it to somebody else anytime soon.
—TOMMY LASORDA

I'd like to be the oldest living actress who's functioning.
—SUSAN SARANDON

I know some guys miss playing and miss it so much it hurts. That is sad. As I said, they ought to get some help. Life has to go on.
—YOGI BERRA

I've seen a lot of men die only a few months after they retire. Sure, working can kill you. But so can not working.
—LEE IACOCCA

Age and Aging

I have trouble with this numbers thing. People are younger than they've ever been, in a sense of energy. They're feeling different. They have a different mind-set.
—GRACE MIRABELLA

This thing with age is just another very superficial way of limiting a person. People develop in different ways. There are some remarkable twenty-year-olds who are so old, and some really stupid fifty-year-olds.
—SUSAN SARANDON

Age is in your head.
—LEO BUSCAGLIA

This is really the best age I've ever encountered. I really know what's happening as far as entertaining an audience. Then to have all this enthusiasm thrown at me—I'm having so much fun, because I know just what to do, which is have a good sense of humor about it. It's just the best time of my life.

  —TONY BENNETT, at sixty-seven, on the secret of his positive attitude

When you're a young man, . . . you're almost helpless in the face of beauty. . . . And when you're very old—or as old as I am [seventy-five], anyway—you still appreciate a beautiful woman, but for one thing: you know you have no shot. And another thing is . . . they have no more surprises.

  —MARIO PUZO

I'm feeling ninety-five.

  —GENE SARAZEN, at ninety-five

Humor

All last year we tried to teach him English, and the only word he learned was *million*.
> —**TOMMY LASORDA**, not at all happy about pitcher Fernando Valenzuela's 1982 salary holdout

I've had a good relationship with police all over the world. I've been stopped, and we've always come to terms.
> —**MARIO ANDRETTI**

It gets late early out here.
> —**YOGI BERRA**, explaining the problem with afternoon shadows in the outfield at Yankee Stadium

Dissension? We got no dissension. What we ain't got is pitchers.
> —**ROY CAMPANELLA**, during a low point for the Brooklyn Dodgers in 1950

Honesty works on the screen and off too. Lying only seems to work when making a deal or reporting your picture's grosses.
—GARRY MARSHALL

It's about as luxurious a life as you can imagine, intellectually. All you have to do is listen, think, conclude, and write. It's heaven. That's one theory. The other theory is: They put you in this big room. They slam this mahogany door shut. And you're dead.
—MARIO CUOMO, on the two views of being a U.S. Supreme Court judge

Carrots might be good for my eyes, but they won't straighten out the curveball.
—CARL FURILLO, baseball player

I feel sorry for people who don't drink, because when they get up in the morning, they're not going to feel any better all day.
—FRANK SINATRA

Never trust a base man who's limping. Comes a base hit, and you'll think he just got back from Lourdes.

—**JOE GARAGIOLA**, baseball player, sportscaster

There goes Rick Monday. He and Manny Mota are so old that they were waiters at the Last Supper.

—**TOMMY LASORDA**, on the two "old men" of the Dodgers

When I go, I'll take New Year's Eve with me.

—**GUY LOMBARDO**

Out of twenty-five guys there should be fifteen who would run through a wall for you, two or three who don't like you at all, five who are indifferent, and maybe three undecided. My job is to keep the last two groups from going the wrong way.

—**BILLY MARTIN**

If you learn to be a perfect singer, you'll end up in the Mormon Tabernacle Choir—with your hands folded.

—**DEAN MARTIN**, to his daughter

So I'm ugly. I never saw anyone hit with his face.
—YOGI BERRA

It isn't that I like the boy because he's Italian. I like
him because I'm Italian.
—JOE PATERNO

Cut me and I'll bleed Dodger blue.
—TOMMY LASORDA

If I had as many love affairs as you have given me
credit for, I would now be speaking to you from a
jar in the Harvard Medical School.
—FRANK SINATRA

I'm not sure I'd rather be managing, or testing bullet-
proof vests.
—JOE TORRE, on being manager of the 1981 Mets

I can't explain the different techniques in Crosby, Sinatra, and me, unless it's that one's bald and one has curly hair and I wear my hair short.
—PERRY COMO

If the people don't want to come out to the park, nobody's going to stop them.
—YOGI BERRA

You know, dear, I've heard a lot of compliments on the coffee. All the guys who smoke say it takes away the nicotine.
—ANGELO DUNDEE, to coffee shop waitress

I've got seven kids. In my house, the three most familiar remarks are "Hello," "good-bye," and "I'm pregnant."
—DEAN MARTIN

Archie didn't elect me [to Congress]—Edith did.
> —GERALDINE FERRARO (1984), on the women's vote in her district in Queens, New York, known as the "Archie Bunker district"

Take Frank first. Then Sammy. Then Bing. Then come back for me. Maybe I just might be ready then.
> —DEAN MARTIN, laughing off the thought of death

I've been married to my wife for forty-two years, to the Dodgers for forty-three.
> —TOMMY LASORDA (1992)

Thanks for coming. If you liked the show, please tell your friends about it. If you didn't, . . . tell them you saw *Cats*.
> —BROOKE SHIELDS, to a *Grease!* audience

I was about ten pounds heavier before I had this accident. You know, you want to lose ten pounds, hit a tree. You'd be surprised—comes right off.
> —TONY DANZA

We got a million good-lookin' guys. But I'm a novelty.
—JIMMY DURANTE

I've always had real good luck with guys from other countries who don't always look where they're supposed to before they throw the ball.
—TOMMY LASORDA, on Japanese Dodgers pitcher Hideo Nomo

It was not too long ago that people thought that semiconductors were part-time orchestra leaders, and microchips were very, very small snack foods.
—GERALDINE FERRARO, on progress

If I get together with two other Italians, it's called Mafia.
—FRANK SINATRA

I didn't know the guy, but I liked his pitchers a lot.
—ROCKY GRAZIANO, when asked if he knew of the painter van Gogh

We have had two chickens in every pot, two cars in every garage, and now we have two headaches for every aspirin.
  —FIORELLO LA GUARDIA

I take Vitamin C. Nuttin' like it!
  —JIMMY DURANTE, on the secret of his powers of attraction

If the rhinestones are turned the wrong way, it'll kill ya.
  —LIBERACE, sitting on his studded coattails

There are three types of baseball players: those who make it happen, those who watch it happen, and those who wonder what happens.
  —TOMMY LASORDA

I suspect that Valium might have been invented to help television producers handle actors. Pro-

zac was created later to help actors deal with producers.
—GARRY MARSHALL

You are not drunk if you can lie on the floor without holding on.
—DEAN MARTIN

Music

He's given us the most mature popular music ever written.
—**TONY BENNETT**, on Frank Sinatra

When I was young, I truly didn't think music had any limitations. I thought it could give you everything you wanted in life.
—**BRUCE SPRINGSTEEN**

There are just certain technical things in music that, if you just listen to it on the gut level and the heart level and the so-on-and-so-forth level, you take it for granted and don't realize what a miracle it is that somebody put it on a piece of paper and then somebody else played it.
—**FRANK ZAPPA**

Now I see that two of the best days of my life were the day I picked up the guitar and the day that I learned how to put it down. Somebody said, "Man, how did you play for so long?" I said: "That's the easy part. It's stopping that's hard."

 —**BRUCE SPRINGSTEEN**, on his devotion to music

The choir was singing, and I could see from the way that the candle flames were wavering that they were responding to the sound waves coming from the choir. That was when I realized that sound, music, had a physical presence and that it could move the air around.

 —**FRANK ZAPPA**, on his realization that "music is, literally, a recipe for sculpted air"

I have a special feeling about the role music should play in a film. I feel that when it's obtrusive or the audience is unduly aware of it, it isn't serving its best purpose.

 —**HENRY MANCINI**, on his belief that "less is better"

Rock 'n' roll is the most brutal, ugly, degenerate, vicious form of expression it has been my displeasure to hear. . . . It fosters almost totally negative and destructive reactions in young people. . . . It is sung, played, and written for the most part by cretinous goons, and by means of its almost imbecilic reiterations and sly, lewd—in plain fact—filthy lyrics, it manages to be the martial music of every sideburned delinquent on the face of the earth.

—FRANK SINATRA

Sexuality

I think we're living in a sexually very repressed society right now. And it's like anything. It's like when you go and everyone is told not to be interested in something, when they're told that it's bad, when they're told that it's taboo, then of course it's human nature to be very interested in it.
—MADONNA

It's a private and intimate thing. And it belongs in that part of the psyche.
--ANNE BANCROFT, on why she doesn't like to talk about sex

I was taught that the denial of desire is one of the foundations of virtue.
—MIRA SORVINO

My love life is what's important to me. That's number one, even before acting.
—AL PACINO

If sexuality means saying yes to life, then you should be able to remain sexual until the day you die.
—SUSAN SARANDON

I have not really been able to put on the screen my own attitudes about eroticism. I have never felt comfortable. Somehow I was never able to set that environment, even for myself. If I was ever able to do that, it could be that I might be able to make a real contribution to erotic film.
—FRANCIS FORD COPPOLA

When you are a virgin longer than other people, you carry around with you a certain pride and vulnerability. My high school boyfriend used to call me the Virgin *Mira*.
—MIRA SORVINO

Money

Volume times zero isn't too healthy.
—**LEE IACOCCA**

In the crush and crunch of cash, it is easy to forget the creative, magic, joyous side [of the creative endeavor] altogether.
—**JOSEPH BARBERA**

I see these guys making millions of dollars, and I wonder, What for? They aren't entrepreneurs. They aren't taking any risk. That's real money we pass on to consumers.
—**JENO PAULUCCI**, on CEO compensation

Big money really does corrupt. It puts a beard on innocence, takes away the edge—the fun, the excite-

ment of suddenly being able to afford certain luxuries. When you can buy anything, the thrill is gone. At least it is for me.
—SYLVESTER STALLONE

Confidence comes from making as much, if not more, money than any studio executive.
—CONNIE STEVENS, actress, entertainer, entrepreneur

I wasn't interested in a snob degree. I was after the bucks.
—LEE IACOCCA

Some ideas develop after days of meetings. Others are born in the flash of a dollar sign set off by a single phone call.
—JOSEPH BARBERA, on how the Flintstones' baby went from being a boy to being a girl

Not to compromise is a marvelous thing to learn. In our kind of materialistic society, our only concern is making money, but you know, you have to keep your integrity to have some peace within yourself.

Just to make money is not enough; that is greedy. Keeping your integrity, you *can* produce and make money. It gives you a quiet dignity and substance. Otherwise, you feel unhappy.

—TONY BENNETT

I don't care nuttin' about money. Sure, I like to think I'm earnin' a buck once in a while. But mostly I just wanna put on a good show.

—JIMMY DURANTE

Food

I love Chinese food, and I also love the food at Twenty One, Romeo Salta, San Marino, and Quo Vadis, and I also love the steak, the Yankee pot roast, the marinated herring, and the roast beef at Toots Shor's.

—**DON AMECHE**, who had a reputation as a gourmand

I cannot understand why people eat so much. . . . I do not like to eat. . . . For me, sometimes a little soup and bread. . . . That is all. I would like to eat *never*.

—**ARTURO TOSCANINI**

Toots Shor's restaurant is so crowded nobody goes there anymore.

—**YOGI BERRA**

Historical Perspective

It was Jack [Maguire] who gave me my nickname of Yogi. Some of us went to a movie with a yogi in it, and afterward Jack began calling me Yogi. It stuck.
   —YOGI BERRA

Once you study the history of art, it's a back door to the history of the world. . . . You never finish learning. It's the adventure of going there that becomes beautiful.
   —TONY BENNETT

I never felt like a pioneer, just a ballplayer.
   —ROY CAMPANELLA, on his role in breaking baseball's color barrier

When the talkies came in, I saw a lot of the actors was hotfooting it to New York for voice lessons. So

I says if you gotta have voice lessons to be an actor, that's for me. So I decided to go to New York.
 —LOU COSTELLO, stage and screen comedian

I loved being at the stadium. I always got there early, and I was never in a rush to leave. We played afternoons then [in the 1930s]. When the game was over, I took my time. Why rush into the night? I used to sit in a room with Pete [Sheehy, the legendary Yankee clubhouse man, who went all the way back to Babe Ruth] and smoke cigarettes and have a few beers and wait until everybody was gone. Sometimes we'd still be there two and three hours after the game. It would get as quiet as a church. I always loved that time of day at Yankee Stadium.
 —JOE DIMAGGIO

I'm glad I did it. If I had it to do over, I would do the same, and that's the end of it.
 —JOHN SIRICA, the Watergate judge

I still wake from time to time in a cold sweat, thinking about what would have happened had I failed to sell *The Flintstones*. It gives me the shivers, too, to think what would have happened if Walt Disney had made good on his promise to call me. Historians of animation speak of the "Nine Old Men" of the Walt Disney Studio. I might have been the tenth. If Disney had called—even if he had phoned me to say, "Look, kid, I can't see you. But if you want to come out to California on your own, well, we'll give you a try,"— I would have quit the bank and hightailed it for Los Angeles. I would have become a painter, filling in the cels with color. I would have graduated to inker, tracing the characters' outlines on the cels. Finally, I might have become an animator—one more anonymous subject of Disney's empire. My work would have been seen by millions, but I would have remained as nameless as if I were still misfiling income tax forms at Irving Trust.

But Disney never called me. And I humbly thank God for that providence.
—JOSEPH BARBERA

There was definitely an attitude when I got here of "Oh, man, what is this world coming to?"
—SONNY BONO

It's strange. Weird. Like it was supposed to happen.
Whenever something did happen, it didn't surprise
us.

—**JOE TORRE**, on the New York Yankees' 1996 World Series win

Through my appearance here today I hope that police officers in the future will not experience the same
frustration and anxiety that I was subjected to for the
past five years at the hands of my superiors because
of my attempts to report corruption.

—**FRANK SERPICO**, at the close of his testimony to the Knapp
Commission

So much of what we do, we think we do it apart
from a history, but we don't. Our history clings to
us, making . . . decisions that we don't realize are
influenced by that history. History is very relevant.

—**GAY TALESE**

The vast, complicated machinery of Hollywood is too
often used to create entertainment for adolescents.
We have perfected our assembly-line methods—but

not the creative processes. We have a magic carpet—
but we don't know how to fly with it.
—**FRANK CAPRA**

Goodnight, Mrs. Calabash, wherever you are.
—**JIMMY DURANTE**'s signature sign-off, probably the best known
in the history of radio and television

Years ago there was a game to popular singing, and
it was a good game. There was an accent on individualism. Kay Starr had her style, Ray Charles had his
style, Sinatra had his style. And each was an individual—a mini-monument. We were fans of one another, and there was a healthy competitiveness. But
then record companies just got greedy. They said,
"Just do songs on the Top Forty." . . . They saw that
there were more people of the Beatles' age group
than any other age group. But I was trained as a
performer before the Beatles. I was trained to play to
the *whole* family, and common sense tells me that is
better business.
—**TONY BENNETT**

You'd see hands sticking out of the mud ... all kinds of broken teacups ... hair sticking out of the road— a quagmire—people don't realize how total the destruction was.

—LAWRENCE FERLINGHETTI, recalling the unforgivable landscape of bombed-out Nagasaki

Insights

We are disgusted by the things we desire and desire what disgusts us.
   —**GOVERNOR MARIO CUOMO**, on television violence

The question of writing is crucial. It is the fundamental pedagogical problem in American education at all levels: How do you get people to write clearly and in an organized fashion? That means nothing other than how do you get them to think clearly.
   —**A. BARTLETT GIAMATTI**

Baseball is ninety percent mental. The other half is physical.
   —**YOGI BERRA**

A game that requires the constant conjuring of animosity.

—**VINCE LOMBARDI**, on football

It has distorted all of the things that we should be getting out of sports. Nobody ever wins a game anymore; somebody else blew it.

—**JOE PATERNO**, referring to sports talk shows

The women's liberation warriors think they have something new, but it's just their armies coming out of the guerrilla hills. Sweet women ambushed men always, at their cradles, in the kitchen, the bedroom.

—**MARIO PUZO**

The Constitution is not an empty bottle. It is like a statue, and the meaning doesn't change.

—**ANTONIN SCALIA**

Comedy's very liberating. It allows you to be less self-conscious and less pristine.

—**BROOKE SHIELDS**

[Some people] come to it through a love of statistics, or the smell of the glove, or just for something that their grandfather recited to them when they were very young. I keep saying: There are many routes to the game. There are many routes to the kingdom of baseball.

    —A. BARTLETT GIAMATTI

Talent must not be wasted. . . . Those who have talent must hug it, embrace it, nurture it, and share it, lest it be taken away as fast as it was loaned to them. Trust me. I've been there.

    —FRANK SINATRA

Failure opens your eyes. When you're flying high, you never learn anything. Only when you *fail* do you pay attention to the problem.

    —SYLVESTER STALLONE

[The average man] doesn't want much. Just peace and freedom, and a break. And he's fundamentally good. If he wasn't, we couldn't hire enough cops to keep him in order.

    —FRANK CAPRA

Steeled in the crucible of suffering, many of the disabled have developed compensatory qualities to offset the extremes of physical makeup.
— HENRY VISCARDI, JR.

Science is the production of new knowledge that can be applied or not, while technology is the application of knowledge to the production of some product, machinery or the like. The two are really very different, and people who have a knack for one very seldom have a knack for the other.
— SALVADOR LURIA

Anyone who is popular is bound to be disliked.
— YOGI BERRA

Men require a challenge. They just have to have it. Whether it's eyeing each other over the seat of a bus or cutting in on somebody who's dancing. They'll go out of their way sometimes to create catastrophe just to prove their mettle. Men have to validate themselves. And when they don't, they live in a netherworld of fertility frustration.
— SYLVESTER STALLONE

Most people think of actors as extraverts, but I believe they go on the stage to overcome their shyness. . . . They enter Sardi's the first time often extremely shy, and it bolsters their ego to have a waiter recognize them and speak to them by name.
—VINCENT SARDI, JR.

The basic ingredient is desire. Because basically when you have the desire, then you find a way, and the motivation is natural. If you have to work yourself to get up for the occasion, then you're wasting energies.
—MARIO ANDRETTI, on what the great ones have

The game isn't over until it's over.
—YOGI BERRA

Life is uncharted territory. It reveals its story one moment at a time.
—LEO BUSCAGLIA

A hunch is creativity trying to tell you something.
—FRANK CAPRA

Mood is not a question of anything logical; it's kind of chemical.
　　—FRANCIS FORD COPPOLA

People want economy, and they will pay any price to get it.
　　—LEE IACOCCA

Everybody needs a hug. It changes your metabolism.
　　—LEO BUSCAGLIA

I have a theory that the only original things we ever do are mistakes.
　　—BILLY JOEL

Statistics are like alienists—they will testify for either side.
　　—FIORELLO LA GUARDIA

If something about another person really, really bothers you and gets under your skin, it elicits a violent

reaction to something in yourself. I absolutely think that's true of me and other people.
—MADONNA

It is not necessary to imagine the world ending in fire or ice. There are two other possibilities: one is paperwork, and the other is nostalgia.
—FRANK ZAPPA

You are classed according to how you look. You may be the best person in the world, but if you go around looking like a bum, you are a bum to other people.
—ROY CAMPANELLA

Mistakes are a part of life; you can't avoid them. All you can hope is that they won't be too expensive and that you don't make the same mistake twice.
—LEE IACOCCA

Working in the entertainment business is like traveling in a foreign country where you don't speak the language. At first, you muddle through with hand

signals, but if you stay there long enough, you can learn to speak the language, or at least learn how to ask where the restroom is.
—GARRY MARSHALL

Don't drink when you drive. Don't even putt.
—DEAN MARTIN

Fashion is about women. It's about what their lives are like and what they are striving to be.
—GRACE MIRABELLA

I firmly believe lifestyle is an art form.
—JOHN TRAVOLTA

I'm an actor, not a star. Stars are people who live in Hollywood and have heart-shaped pools.
—AL PACINO

Asking questions and challenging things is the way things get defined.
—SUSAN SARANDON

The amount of damage that has been done, over the years, by love songs is almost incalculable, because a love song creates the desire for a situation which will never be created in real life, so it just breeds frustration. A kid grows up listening to love songs, and he is comparing his life to what is being talked about on the record. And he ain't never gonna get it, you know, so it mutates him.
    —FRANK ZAPPA

We're all boat people. . . . The Italians were boat people. . . . But the Haitians, the people from the Orient, the Koreans that are serving us fruit—they're all part of this same thing of being Americans.
    —GAY TALESE

Comedy may be many things to many people. But one thing it is not to anybody; it is not a tragic ending.
    —FRANK CAPRA

You can't lose the chance to splurge on getting to know people.
    —JOHN TRAVOLTA

There is . . . much more to the collapse of assumed social normalities than a TV set. The blood and bone of a durable society is formed by how the citizens of a nation conduct themselves among daily moral challenges.
—JACK VALENTI

The function of the critic is insight. If the critic has not intuition, he has nothing.
—LAWRENCE FERLINGHETTI

People who have perfect-looking outsides don't always have perfectly matching insides.
—GARRY MARSHALL

Film is about lines painted on the floor. The stage is a high-wire act a hundred feet up.
—AL PACINO

There is more stupidity around than hydrogen, and it has a longer shelf life.
—FRANK ZAPPA

People who are looking for art in rock 'n' roll or pop are looking for something that either doesn't or shouldn't exist there. An artist is a guy with a beret who sits in a park and paints pictures, and he starves in a garret somewhere.
    —BILLY JOEL

To me a family value has to do with old-fashioned words like "honor" and "duty" and "service" and "compassion" and "pride" and "sacrifice."
    —JACK VALENTI

If Truth Be Told . . .

I figure I was put on this earth to drive race cars.
—**MARIO ANDRETTI**

At least seventy percent of all racehorses don't want to win.
—Attributed to **EDDIE ARCARO**

I am not a bully. I can't help it if people use my name in that manner, but I don't operate that way. Have I made recommendations? Yes! And if people accept them, fine!
—**ALFONSE D'AMATO**

My accident took me out for a year, and I worked four hours a day, six days a week, to get back. When

people ask how it changed me, I tell them, "Well, I got over my mid-life crisis just like *that*." But the injury made me think about all the things I dreamed of doing.
　—TONY DANZA

I did naughty things. There was a time [when I was in my thirties] when I wanted to see an X-rated movie, okay? I bought a blond wig. And I got into the movie. . . . It was boring.
　—ANNETTE FUNICELLO

I'm not a show-biz guy. I have to smell the sweatshirts.
　—JOE GARAGIOLA

I don't know that I have a choice. The only way I could be less combative would be if I would compromise more. If I compromised more, I would achieve less.
　—RUDOLPH GIULIANI

It's a combat zone.

—**LEE IACOCCA**, then president of Ford Motor Company

I have no desire to be a "pop" singer. Opera attracts me most, because it's on stage. I guess I'm a ham at heart.

—**ANNA MOFFO**

People don't credit me with much of a brain, so why should I disillusion them?

—**SYLVESTER STALLONE**

I know the elbow will be much better because of this. But damn it, sometimes I'd rather just go out and throw, and if the darn thing tears off, it tears off.

—**JOE MONTANA**, impatiently waiting out his four-week injured-reserve status in 1992

Billiards is a great tranquilizer for the harried executive and anxious housewife, but for the tournament player it can be real torture.

—**WILLIE MOSCONI**

The stupidity of brilliant people never ceases to amaze me.
—JENO PAULUCCI

I'd rather be a swing man on a championship team than a regular on another team.
—LOU PINIELLA, baseball player

If a novelist goes out to Hollywood to work on his book, he has to accept the fact that it's not his movie. And the truth is that if I had been bossing the making of the movie [*The Godfather*], I would have wrecked it. Directing a movie is an art, or a craft.
—MARIO PUZO

I didn't wait my whole life for this game. I waited for the series.
—JOE TORRE, after the Yankees' 12–1 loss in game one of the 1996 World Series

I'm not going to be Bill Clinton and say I never inhaled. I did inhale. I liked tobacco a lot better.
—FRANK ZAPPA

Some actors hide, but I know that the real reason for getting into the business is to get loved. I want to be loved. . . . I want to be loved by the greatest number of people it is humanly possible to be loved by.
—DANNY AIELLO

Jocks are little guys, and most little guys don't have it their way. They start getting up on horses, and, after a while, they learn to manage those animals, and then they've got twelve hundred pounds going for them, and it makes them as big as the biggest guy.
—EDDIE ARCARO

Performing is always under stress, . . . because you want to please the people.
—LIZA MINNELLI

It's a great game, but it's not much fun anymore. There are only about ten real pros in pocket billiards—only five who are first-class. All the rest are a lazy bunch of louts.
—WILLIE MOSCONI

Streaks don't go on forever. Some fans might think they do, but they don't.
—JOE PATERNO

You know, a lot of people think I'm always arguing with the umpires when I turn around, but actually I'm not. I'm just talking conversation to them.
—YOGI BERRA

[Being a mayor] is the hardest political job there is—there's no insulation. You do something bad, you pay for it the next day.
—SONNY BONO (1991)

When I sell liquor, it's called bootlegging; when my patrons serve it on silver trays on Lake Shore Drive, it's called hospitality.
—AL CAPONE

Modern art is what happens when painters stop looking at girls and persuade themselves that they have a better idea.
—JOHN CIARDI

I grew up thinking that I was Italian. But after living in Italy, I realized that I was American. Now I consider myself—and am proud to be—Italian-American!
  —**BILL CONTI**, composer and conductor

Everything you've ever read about or seen on TV, I've done it for real.
  —**ANTHONY DELLAVENTURA**

A lot of people don't like to look at themselves on the screen. But I've got an ego you can't fit in this room. So, since I love myself so much, I can tolerate even the worst work.
  —**DANNY DEVITO**

I guess without my proboscitor [nose], I'd be just another mortal.
  —**JIMMY DURANTE**

I like New York. I always liked it. It is a living city. . . . It is like strong wine.
  —**ARTURO TOSCANINI**

Like a dime among pennies.
—Five-foot-two-inch **FIORELLO LA GUARDIA**, on how it feels to
be the smallest man in a group

The uniform is not going to change you. If you're a
crook before you put it on, you're still a crook.
Worse, you'll be a hypocrite.
—**FRANK SERPICO**, in a lecture to police officers

I'm not a right-wing jingoistic human being. Rambo
is. He's psychotic in many ways.
—**SYLVESTER STALLONE**

Now we've got someone our fans can really hate.
—Hockey player **PHIL ESPOSITO**, welcoming the NHL's Miami
  expansion team

I didn't know I was part Italian until I became
famous.
—**FRANCO HARRIS**, on the fact that little attention had been given
  to his ethnic origin

I was destined to play Evita.
—MADONNA

The Constitution gives every American the inalienable right to make a damn fool of himself.
—JOHN CIARDI

It is a little building with big scale, surrounded by big buildings with little scale.
—ROBERT VENTURI, on his creation, the Seattle Art Museum

Everything I do is personal.
—GAY TALESE, on self-revelation

The phone wasn't exactly ringing off the hook. So I thought, I want to stay in this game [hockey], but why the hell do I have to be cold?
—PHIL ESPOSITO, on why he chose Tampa

When I was very young, I kissed my first woman and smoked my first cigarette on the same day. Be-

lieve me, never since have I wasted any more time on tobacco.
—ARTURO TOSCANINI

Listening to all that stuff
Must have made them crazy.
I can't believe I said
All those things.
—PHIL RIZZUTO, on the publication of his on-air meditations